What Is Lightning?

Weather Wise

by Ellen Lawrence

Consultant:

Jeffrey B. Basara, PhD
Associate Professor, School of Meteorology
University of Oklahoma
Norman, Oklahoma

BEARPORT
PUBLISHING

New York, New York

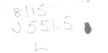
Credits

Cover, © ChaNaWit/Shutterstock; 3, © Sytillin Pavel/Shutterstock; 4–5, © Balazs Kovacs Images/Shutterstock; 6, © Dmytro Kosmenko/Shutterstock, © kzww/Shutterstock, and © Julia Ivantsova/Shutterstock; 7, © Eye Ubiquitous/Alamy; 8, © Nature Picture Library/Alamy; 9, © ChaNaWit/Shutterstock; 10, © Gayvoronskaya Yana/Shutterstock; 11, © Keith Homan/Shutterstock; 12, © Danita Delimont/Alamy; 13, © NASA/Luca Parmitano; 14, © swal82/Shutterstock; 15, © Balazs Kovacs Images/Shutterstock; 16, © wavebreakmedia/Shutterstock; 17, © Shutterstock and Ruby Tuesday Books; 18, © Gdragan/IstockPhoto; 19, © S-F/Shutterstock; 19R, © Paul Souders/Corbis; 20, © Jon Bilous/Shutterstock; 21, © liseykina/Shutterstock; 22, © Gelpi JM/Shutterstock, © Dmitri Malyshev/Shutterstock, and © exopixel/Shutterstock; 23TL, © Prasit Rodphan/Shutterstock; 23TC, © Mihai Simonia/Shutterstock; 23TR, © Julia Ivantsova/Shutterstock; 23BL, © Dmytro Vietrov/Shutterstock; 23BC, © Luis Molinero/Shutterstock; 23BR, © A Lesik/Shutterstock.

Publisher: Kenn Goin
Editor: Jessica Rudolph
Creative Director: Spencer Brinker
Design: Emma Randall
Photo Researcher: Ruby Tuesday Books Ltd.

Library of Congress Cataloging-in-Publication Data

Lawrence, Ellen, 1967– author.
 What is lightning? / by Ellen Lawrence.
    pages cm — (Weather wise)
 Includes bibliographical references and index.
 Audience: 7–12.
 ISBN 978-1-62724-863-1 (library binding) — ISBN 1-62724-863-3 (library binding)
 1. Lightning—Juvenile literature. 2. Thunderstorms—Juvenile literature. I. Title. II. Series:
Lawrence, Ellen, 1967– Weather wise.
 QC966.5.L39 2016
 551.56'32—dc22
                          2015017490

For more information, write to Bearport Publishing Company, Inc., 45 West 21st Street, Suite 3B, New York, New York 10010. Printed in the United States of America.

10 9 8 7 6 5 4 3 2 1

Contents

Flash! Bang!

It's a hot summer evening and a thunderstorm has begun.

The sky is filled with huge, dark clouds, and raindrops are starting to fall from the sky.

Suddenly, a jagged flash of light shoots from the clouds. It's lightning!

Within seconds, thunder fills the air with loud bangs.

What do you think causes lightning?

It's possible to see lightning from 100 miles (161 km) away.

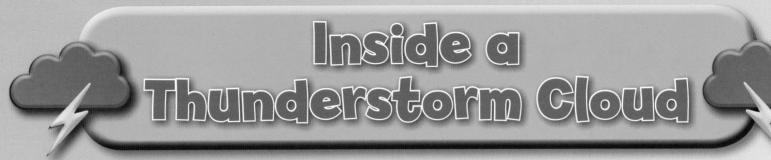

Lightning is created inside a thunderstorm cloud. How?

First, a cloud forms from billions of tiny droplets of water.

The cloud grows bigger and moves higher in the sky, where the air is very cold.

Then, ice **crystals** form in the cloud and mix with the droplets of water.

The crystals and water droplets move constantly.

As they move, something amazing happens in the cloud.

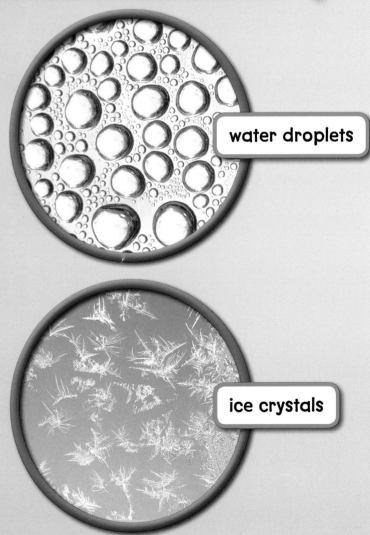

water droplets

ice crystals

The type of cloud where a thunderstorm forms is called a cumulonimbus (*kyoo*-myuh-loh-NIHM-buss) cloud. It may be several miles wide and 10 miles (16 km) tall!

cumulonimbus cloud

A Giant Spark

In the thunderstorm cloud, the moving ice crystals crash into each other.

All of this movement creates **electricity**.

The amount of electricity grows and grows until a giant spark is created.

This huge, bright spark is the lightning flash, or **bolt**, that lights up the sky.

Sometimes during a lightning strike, we cannot see the bolt's jagged lines in the sky. However, the thunderstorm cloud will still light up.

Where Does It Go?

Most bolts of lightning are formed inside and strike within a single cloud.

This is called intracloud lightning.

Sometimes, however, lightning travels toward the ground.

In an instant, it strikes the first thing it can reach.

Often, this is a tall tree or building.

intracloud lightning

About three quarters of all lightning is intracloud lightning. The remainder of lightning bolts hit the ground or something on the ground, such as a tall building.

lightning striking buildings

Super Fast, Super Hot

Lightning travels very quickly.

Each bolt flashes for less than a second.

Lightning is also extremely hot.

A bolt of lightning heats the air around it to about 54,000°F (29,982°C).

That's five times hotter than the surface of the Sun!

What do you think causes the thunder we hear after a flash of lightning?

lightning at the Grand Canyon

A Clap of Thunder

Soon after lightning occurs, a clap of thunder is heard.

What causes this loud noise?

As a lightning bolt travels through the sky, it forces the air around it to **vibrate**—really fast.

As the air vibrates, it makes lots of noise.

We hear this noise as the bangs, booms, and rumbles of thunder.

Sometimes during a thunderstorm, the ice crystals and water droplets in a storm cloud combine. They form large chunks of ice that fall to Earth. These ice chunks are called hailstones.

hailstones

Lightning and Thunder

lightning

a few seconds later . . .

clap of thunder

Hold a ruler at one end, then quickly wave it up and down. The whoosh noise you hear is the air vibrating. The movement of the ruler makes the air vibrate—just like a lightning bolt does.

# Listen for the Bang

The noise of thunder is made by a lightning bolt.

So why don't we see lightning and hear thunder at exactly the same time?

The reason is that light and sound travel at different speeds.

When a lightning bolt flashes, the light reaches our eyes almost instantly.

However, it takes the sound of thunder longer to reach our ears.

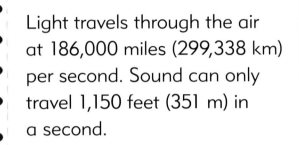

Light travels through the air at 186,000 miles (299,338 km) per second. Sound can only travel 1,150 feet (351 m) in a second.

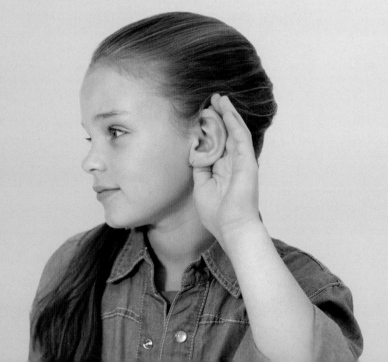

It's possible to figure out how far away a thunderstorm is. Watch for a lightning flash. Then count how many seconds pass before you hear thunder. It takes about 5 seconds for the noise of thunder to travel 1 mile (1.6 km). So, if you count 10 seconds, the storm is 2 miles (3.2 km) away.

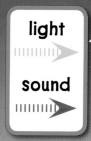

light

sound

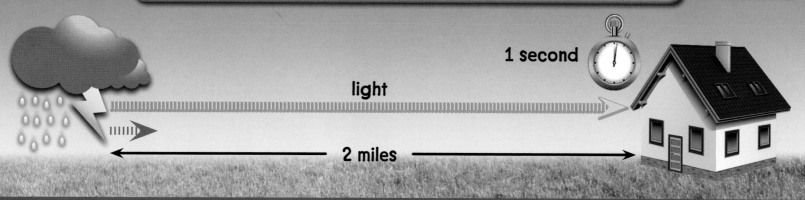

1 second

light

2 miles

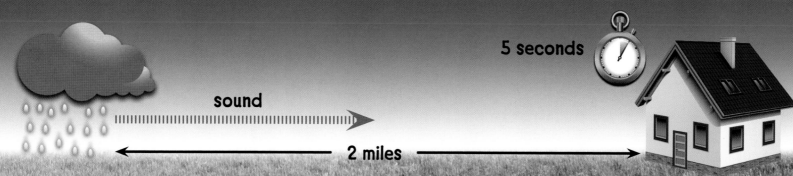

5 seconds

sound

2 miles

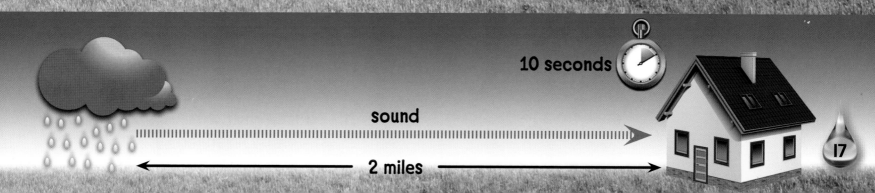

10 seconds

sound

2 miles

17

Are Thunderstorms Dangerous?

Most thunderstorms aren't dangerous, but lightning may cause harm.

If lightning strikes a tree, the tree can catch fire.

This may cause a **wildfire**.

Also, it's rare, but sometimes people are struck by lightning.

People who are hit by lightning may get seriously injured or be killed.

a tree that was struck by lightning

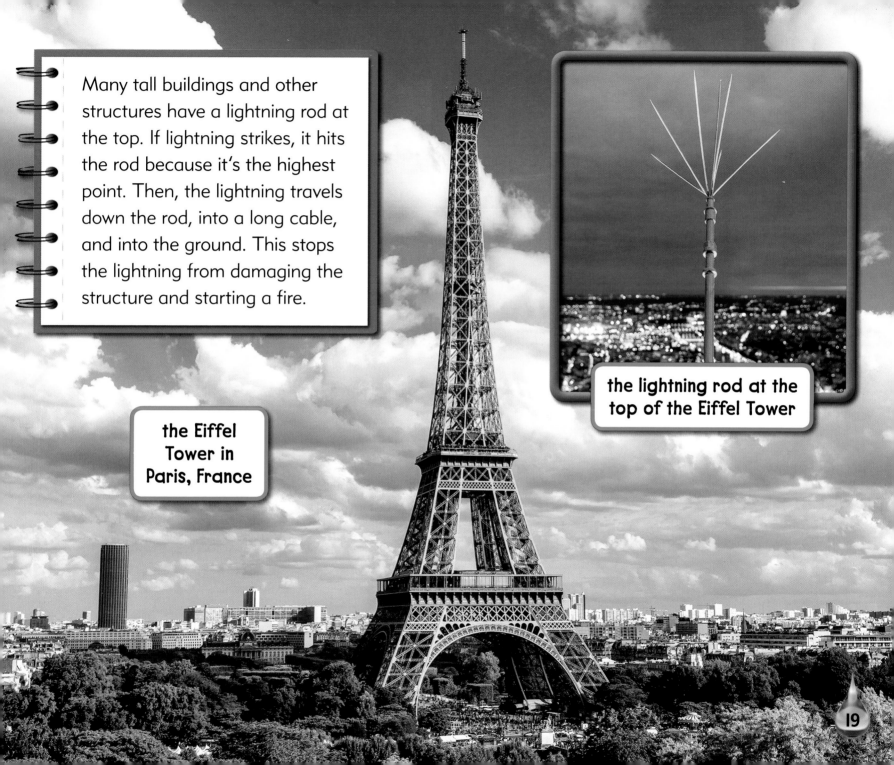

Many tall buildings and other structures have a lightning rod at the top. If lightning strikes, it hits the rod because it's the highest point. Then, the lightning travels down the rod, into a long cable, and into the ground. This stops the lightning from damaging the structure and starting a fire.

the Eiffel Tower in Paris, France

the lightning rod at the top of the Eiffel Tower

19

Being Weather-Wise

It's important to stay safe during thunderstorms.

If dark storm clouds appear or you hear distant thunder, move indoors.

When there's no building nearby, you can sit in a car, but keep the windows closed.

Never take shelter under a tree, though, because the tree may **attract** lightning.

Stay indoors until the storm is over, and you'll be dry, safe, and weather-wise!

dark storm clouds

At any moment, there are about 2,000 thunderstorms happening around the world.

Science Lab

Make a Spark of Lightning

Is it possible to make a spark similar to lightning using a balloon and a metal spoon? Let's investigate!

1. Blow up a balloon.

2. Take the balloon and the spoon into a dark room.

3. Rub the balloon against your hair for two minutes.

4. Slowly and carefully, move the balloon toward the spoon.

   • *What do you observe happening?*

   • *What did you create when you rubbed the balloon on your hair?*

   • *How is what happened in your experiment similar to what happens during a thunderstorm?*

   (See answers on page 24.)

Science Words

attract (uh-TRAKT) cause something to be pulled near

bolt (BOLT) another word for a flash of lightning

crystals (KRISS-tuhlz) tiny pieces of ice that have formed into shapes that have straight edges and smooth sides

electricity (i-lek-TRISS-uh-tee) a kind of energy that is used to make heat and light and to power machines

vibrate (VYE-brayt) to move back and forth very quickly; when air vibrates, this makes sounds we hear with our ears

wildfire (WILDE-fire) a fire that spreads quickly over a large area, usually in the wilderness

Index

Read More

Edison, Erin. *Lightning (Weather Basics)*. Mankato, MN: Capstone (2012).

Green, Jen. *Weather and Seasons (Our Earth)*. New York: Rosen (2008).

Lawrence, Ellen. *What Is Weather? (Weather Wise)*. New York: Bearport (2012).

Learn More Online

To learn more about lightning and thunder, visit **www.bearportpublishing.com/WeatherWise**

About the Author

Ellen Lawrence lives in the United Kingdom. Her favorite books to write are those about animals and nature. In fact, the first book Ellen bought for herself, when she was six years old, was the story of a gorilla named Patty Cake that was born in New York's Central Park Zoo.

Answers for Page 22

When you rubbed the balloon on your hair, you created a type of electricity called static electricity. The electricity made a spark that was attracted to the spoon. Just as the ice crystals in a cloud crash into each other and make electricity, the balloon and your hair made electricity when they were rubbed together. Then the electricity spark struck the spoon, just like a bolt of lightning strikes objects on the ground.